William Rand   2019

William Rand studio in Blue Hill, 1981.

FERRETERIA VASCO=MADRILEÑA

José Carlos Zubillaga Vázquez   D. N. I. 732.476 - H

ESPECIALIDAD EN TODA CLASE DE HERRAMIENTAS
SUMINISTROS A OBRAS Y TALLERES

42, INFANTAS, 42 - TELEFONO 91 521 30 86

Madrid, 17 de 9 de 1998

RAND, WM.

D. N. I. o C. I. F.

		PRECIO	TOTAL
1	*taladro Bosch*		9990
1	*juego brocas*		850
2	*Rogueta Panflex*		100
2	*caja encaje*		200

FERRETERIA VASCO MADRILEÑA
Calle Infantas, 42
Telf. 221 30 86 - MADRID-4

Mistress Debra Tripodi, William Rand
and waiter (slave) at La Nouvelle Justine
(S+M restaurant) East Village,
New York, 1998

Chupitos, 1997
Oil on six canvases, assembled
84" x 60"

Ava Gardner Breakfast, 2000
Oil on canvas
24" x 36"

William Baker Rand 617

I think that art is something that should be grand. My paintings are always as big as Steinway pianos. My interest in large scale is my ongoing revolt against Colonial New England, because they won't fit in a Colonial house.

William Rand

From childhood Rand was familiar with
the photo his father had taken of a
US Air Force plane in Okinawa with its
provocative pin-up girl. The fusion
of war and sex has been a theme in his
art ever since.

(see page 60, *Blut und Boden*,
at Colby College Museum of Art, 1993).

Height precedes width for
artwork dimensions.

Foreward

For two centuries Maine has nurtured its artists, both those who live here as well as those from "away." Beginning with landscapist Charles Codman's arrival in Portland from Boston in 1822, the state has been a haven for some of America's most creative painters, sculptors, and photographers. Here amid a rugged topography of great natural beauty, they have found a place of independent spirit and respect for individual expression.

William Rand had the good fortune to grow up in Maine, received his artistic education here, and launched his painting career in the coastal village of Blue Hill. From the 1980s until recently, he has painted in New York City, Berlin, and Spain, reminiscent of the nineteenth century Maine sculptors Paul Akers and Franklin Simmons, who spent much of their lives in Italy.

Debbie, New York, 1994

Like fellow Mainer Marsden Hartley did in 1937, William Rand has now returned to the state to pursue his work. This striking book is a celebration of four decades of his paintings. Presented chronologically, the pictures on these pages bear witness to a remarkable journey of artistic exploration. While the theme of the human form rendered in black and white is ever-present, the wide range of subjects and the varied ways in which they are depicted provide an ever-unfolding kaleidoscope of powerful images. From the graceful elegance of the eighteenth century *Blindfolded Draftsman* to the cruel reality of slavery in *The Long Walk*, William is fearless in committing his inquiring intellect to canvas. He does so by freely using realism and historical and literary references in his desire to reach his viewers.

It should come as no surprise that one of William Rand's ancestors was the nineteenth century landscape painter Roswell Morse Shurtleff, who befriended Winslow Homer during the Civil War and later introduced him to the Adirondacks. In 1883 Homer settled at Prout's Neck on the Maine coast, where he began the most significant phase of his career. Likewise, may Maine now provide the setting for chapters yet unwritten in the book of William Rand's art.

Earle G. Shettleworth, Jr.
Maine State Historian
April, 2018

Winslow Homer
The Angler (Casting in the Falls -
Portrait of Roswell Morse Shurtleff), ca. 1874
Oil on canvas
23.375" x 17.125"
Fine Arts Museums of San Francisco
De Young & Legion of Honor
Collection of Bernard Osher

Perry's Nut House, Post Card,
Courtesy Earle G. Shettleworth Jr.
and Maine Historic Preservation
Commission

Text from back of post card:

*Most Interesting Place
On the Maine Coast.*

*To you who enter this place,
we who manage this Nut House
extend you a hearty greeting.
We want you to feel that this is a
human house and not a soulless
institution.*

*Perry's Tropical Nut House
East Belfast, Maine*

William Rand left his ancestral home on the coast of Maine, where his forbears had been seafarers and shipbuilders, for the heady downtown scene of 1980s New York, and from there to Berlin and later Spain. Now in his sixth decade, Rand has come full circle back to his roots. It makes sense that he would find common chord with Marsden Hartley's late career embrace of nativism as the two artists share a similar peripatetic path. Rand's work, like Hartley's, is deeply autobiographical. He says simply, "Maine is where my heart is."

A marvelous raconteur, brilliant draftsman, and sharp-eyed, searing documentarian, Rand's grand-scale black and white paintings chronicle his life and our times. Drawn from eclectic sources — art history, geopolitics, literature, sports, nature, pop culture, current events — his imagery seduces with its intoxicating mix of beauty and decadence, highbrow and lowbrow. We want to be at this party.

Rand's parents were "in-tune with cultural shifts," cultured and hip. His mother was a leader in Maine's historic preservation movement, and his father was a cartographer and the State geologist. They encouraged the boy's interest in art and introduced him to museums at an early age. But he especially liked Perry's Nuthouse in Belfast, a tourist attraction that housed a vast collection of taxidermy animals and nuts from around the world.

While studying at the Portland School of Art in the 1970s, Rand became acquainted with Fluxus artist Albert M. Fine, who convinced him to abandon color. But the roots of Rand's affinity for black and white lie in the television of his childhood and the hundreds of hours he spent poring over a first edition of Charles Adams's black and white drawings. By the time he left art school in the late 1970s, he was committed to this aesthetic.

When Rand's father, a lifelong sailor, died in 2007, the son painted *Osprey*, now in the collection of the Portland Museum of Art. This testament, which depicts his father's favorite bird, acknowledges death's merciless stalking.

"Seafaring people always have a divided heart," says Rand, acknowledging the conflict between his Yankee roots and his need to roam.

Osprey, 2007
Charcoal, ink, latex and varnish on canvas
56" x 58"
Portland Museum of Art, Maine.
Gift of William Rand
in memory of his father John R. Rand

Europe offered Rand new horizons and the anonymity to come to terms with his sexuality, as it did for Hartley decades before. Living abroad, he painted in the "non-stop and pleasure-mad" milieux of Berlin, Madrid, and the Spanish Mediteranean, where he lived successively for twenty years before returning to Maine in 2016.

Rand's paintings from Europe straddle the sacred and profane. Every strata of society is breached as models from brothels, the street, and European royalty are treated without distinction. The specter of war hovers throughout. Particularly representative is the one-hundred-foot long, modular *The Ava Gardner Project,* which occupied the artist between 2000 and 2003 in Madrid.

Desire and longing, glamour and decay, violence and love are the recurring themes in Rand's art: the need for connection, for belonging. He writes, "For me, painting is about fighting loneliness in the world. Paintings don't leave you like lovers do, paintings don't die like friends. Each painting is a special friend to keep me company."

In his art, William Rand strips the veneer from who we think we are to show us as we are. His paintings are timeless revelations of human frailty, passion, and endurance. We are seduced by their beauty, moved by their humanity, and grateful to the artist for holding up the mirror.

Suzette McAvoy
Director
Center for Maine Contemporary Art
November, 2017

William Rand, 1976

1953

William Rand is born in Michigan. He grows up on the Maine coast, where he is tutored in art and avidly explores the natural world.

1960s

As a teenager, Rand studies Pre-Raphaelite painting in England and is influenced by the bold graphics of contemporary record album cover art.

1970s

Rand studies human anatomy, drawing, sculpture, design, and painting, including Bauhaus color theory, at the Portland School of Art (now MECA).

1978

He meets Fluxus master Albert M. Fine and receives covert Fluxus lessons, beginning with the elimination of color in his work. Rand graduates with a BFA in painting.

1979

Rand moves to Blue Hill and paints large monochromatic canvases in an abandoned, unheated, dockside granite building. Against large, thickly painted black grounds, the figure becomes a central element in his work.

1980s and 1990s

Rand paints and exhibits in both Maine and New York.

1981

Boston's Gallery East hosts *William Rand Major Paintings* exhibition

1983

Rand is represented in *Maine Artist's Invitational* at the Bowdoin College Museum of Art in Brunswick.

National and International Events

1951
The world meets Holden Caulfield when J.D. Salinger's publishes *Catcher in the Rye*.

1956
Elvis Presley's *Heartbreak Hotel* tops the Billboard charts.

1961
Construction of the Berlin Wall begins in East Germany.

1964
Three thousand Beatles fans welcome Pan Am flight 101 at JFK Airport.

1967
A sit-in by welfare mothers sparks race riots in Roxbury, Massachusetts.

1970
President Richard M. Nixon orders an invasion of Cambodia, expanding the war in Southeast Asia.

1973
Pablo Picasso dies in Mougins, France at age 91

1982
Anselm Kiefer paintings are shown at Mary Boone Gallery, New York

William Baker Rand 16|17

Top: William Rand, Calderwood Building, Portland School of Art, 1977

Bottom: William Rand in pool, with studio in background, Blue Hill, Maine, 1979

Top: Anthony Gaskin, Blue Hill, Maine, 1996

Middle: *Portrait of Pat Hearn; Dorsal View*, 1984, 36" x 36," oil on canvas

Bottom: Paintings in studio, Blue Hill, Maine, 1985

Below: Pat Hearn and William Rand, Blue Hill, Maine, 1981

Bottom: William Rand and Anthony Gaskin, New Meadows River, Maine, 2003

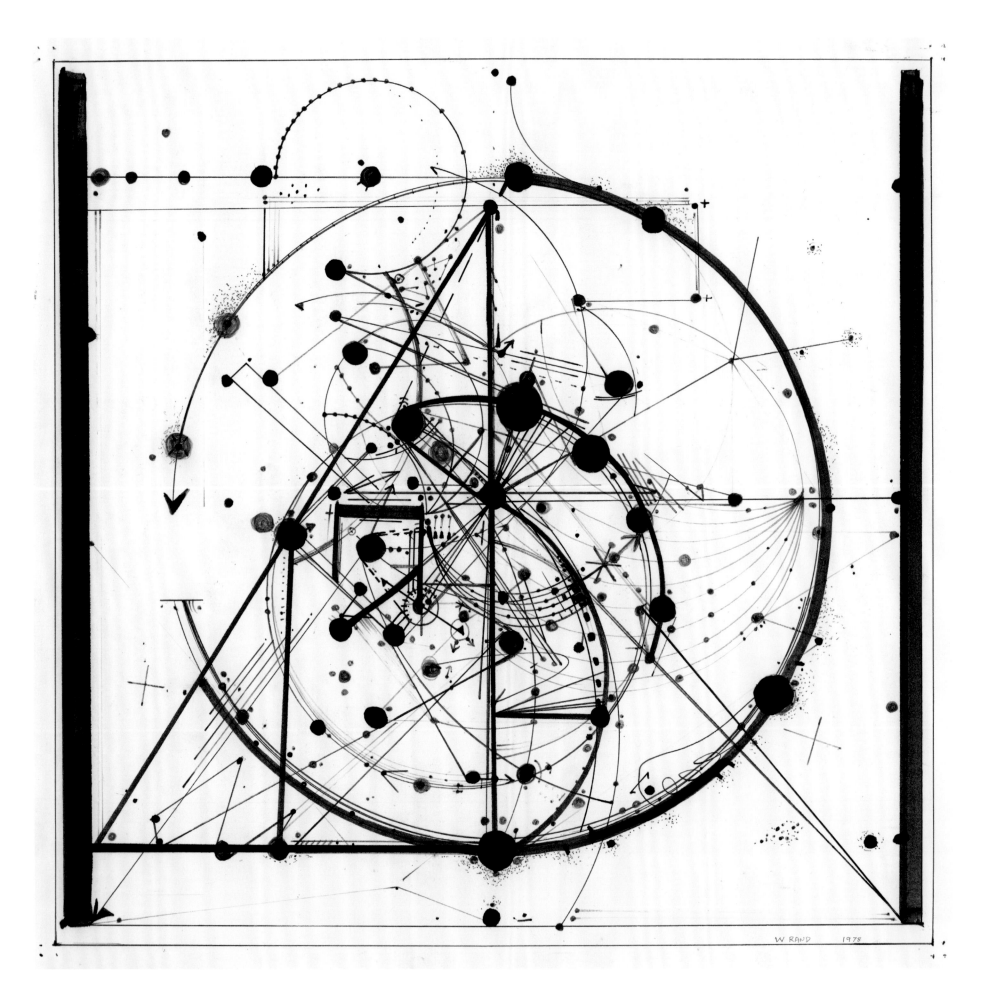

W RAND   1978

Unafraid to reminisce on
or with the past,
and to slap,
with a perfectly dead cod,
the immediacy of the present
in the face with it.

Albert M. Fine, composer, artist, and poet

Opposite:
Fluxus drawing, 1978
Ink on paper
10" x 10"

Empty House by the Sea, 1980
Oil on canvas
84" x 72"

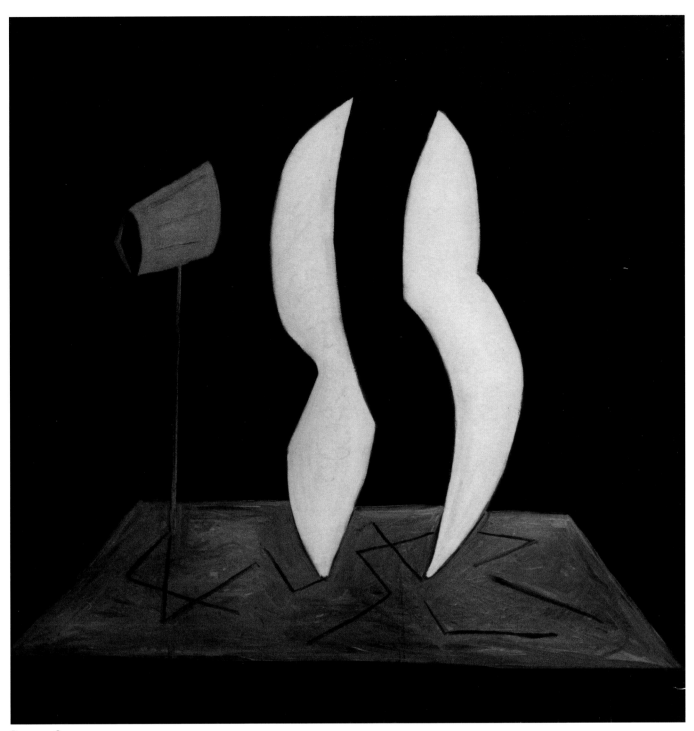

Danse, 1981
Oil on canvas
72" x 72"
(Destroyed)

Silence, 1981
Oil on canvas
72" x 72"

Silence was used on the invitation to the
exhibition *William Rand Major Paintings*
at Gallery East in Boston, 1981

Opposite:
Blue Hill, 1981

Granite studio, Blue Hill, Maine, 1982

William Rand of Blue Hill is a strong, insistent painter who is not out to beguile the viewer. By building a rigorous aesthetic founded mostly on tones of grey and a bold monolithic geometry, he has contributed the most arresting pictures in the show. These are stout-hearted paintings in tone, form and content.

Philip M. Isaacson
Portland Press Herald
Maine Artist's Invitational
Bowdoin College Museum of Art, 1983

Opposite:
Untitled, 1982
Oil on canvas
72" x 72"
Private Collection, New York

Painting in the Granite Building
Blue Hill, Maine

William Rand in the granite studio in
Blue Hill, Maine, 1984

Black oil paint does not freeze in the studio on the water in Maine during the coldest months.

Wrapped in a ski parka, gloves, hat and boots I paint and draw in sub-zero weather.
An audible silence is the air inside the stone room praying.
Frost sprays across the glass in sparkling indigo daybreak.

The frozen wooden boards under foot crunch and snap as I walk across the vast space
to light a fire.

Painting large turgid empty black areas on canvases with a brush and crushing the brushstrokes
with a painter´s knife, I stand far away and listen to the roar of the winter winds blowing snow
across the dry frozen white landscape, and there the currents gnaw at the studio door.

Hard glistening lights reflect in the turgid waves chopping up the harbour, sending dreamy
splattered flashes of coloured light through the tall glass front doors and high across the granite
blocks like wild birds.
And still I paint in black.

Returning at night, I mash up the hard white zinc oxide oil paint near a light bulb and fill in the
knife etched forms on the black canvases, forms based upon the marble ruins tumbling about in
the mind from an autumnal expedition to Athens sketching in the ancient Athenian Agora on
Greek newspapers.

The slinking wise half mad cats of the Parthenon ease between the crevices of a lost ancient
civilization where the world breaks in two.
Unheard voices whisper beyond the Delphic mists.

WILLIAM RAND, 1982

Opposite:
Empty House by the Sea, 1980
Pencil on bristol
28" x 28"

Drill, 1984
Oil on canvas
48" x 60"
Private Collection

Opium, 1985
Oil on canvas
48" x 60"
Private Collection

Granite studio, Blue Hill, Maine, 1985

Man rowing, 1984
Oil on canvas
48" x 48"

Opposite:
Trapeze (for Thos. Dewing), 1985
Oil on canvas
72" x 72"

Corner in Paris, 1986
Oil on canvas
60" x 72"

Opposite:
William Rand and models, downtown
Blue Hill, Maine garage studio, 1986

Titania and Bottom, 1986
Oil on canvas
60" x 120"
Private Collection, St. Louis

Passing Ships, 1990
Oil and shellac on dropcloth
59" x 59"

This painting was included in a 1990

The entire oeuvre of William Rand deals precisely in the larger examples of contemporary high art. Gustave Courbet in the nineteenth century declared that true artists can only be of their times and paint what is real. In each of Rand's explosive episodes the denouement retroactively relates to tangible circumstances of these times. The deprogramming this artist subjected himself to is essential to the understanding of his vernacular.

Like the stealthiness of the *Road Warrior*, he offers his audience the Hardcore Truth of existence in the modern world.

Dennis Adamo, art and media critic
For Those About to Rock
William Rand Exhibition catalog
Colby College Museum of Art, Waterville, Maine, 1993

William Rand Exhibition
Colby College Museum of Art, 1993

The Blindfolded Draughtsman, 2005
Oil on canvas
48" x 60"
Private Collection, Maine

William Rand in welding studio, 2007

The Naughty Ballerina, 2005
Oil on canvas
72" x 60"
Private Collection, Maine

William Rand, Hopkins Island, 2000

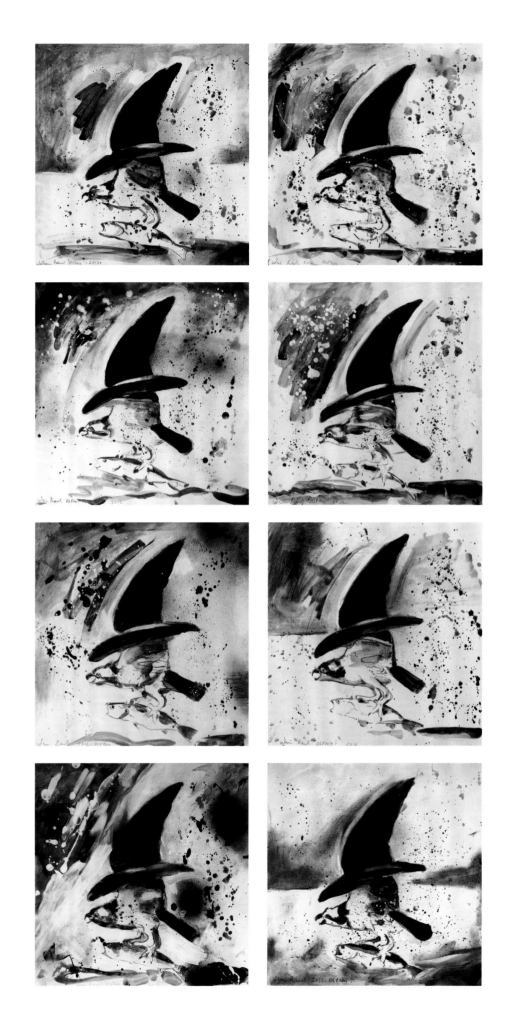

Osprey I, II, III, V, VII, IX, 2012
Varnished paint on paper
11.75" x 11.75"

Opposite:
River God (detail), 1991
Gesso, charcoal, acrylic, and oil on canvas
58" x 72"
Private Collection, New York

THIS SHOULDN'T BE SEXY

YET IT IS

Rene Ricard

William Rand Downtown

In the New York of the 80s and 90s, the legendary 3rd floor studio of William Rand on the corner of 1st and 1st was a magnet for artists, writers, and collectors. We were drawn to a long table strewn with wine glasses, drawings, slides of paintings, books, plates of pasta and clams, and candelabra blazing, surrounded by people with huge appetites, consuming art and food.

The downtown setting was just an extension of the canvas on which William Rand was working. Originally from Maine, he would orchestrate seating so that the society matron from Bar Harbor might find herself in conversation with the famous but homeless poet, and discover that he too had been born in Lewiston. Whether the revelation would result in a screaming match or a love-fest was never certain, and Rand loved that dissonant edge.

While we were thus engaged, the artist would paint. Some artists find inspiration in the solitude of a quiet atelier, but for William Rand, the chaos in his studio fueled him. The work that emerged occupies the delicate space between raw and defined, controlled and chaotic.

Bill Stelling, FUN Gallery,
New York, 1990

Imagining his Madrid studio of later years, I picture a similar scene, perhaps one involving a transexual channeling Ava Gardner, or a handsome matador recovering from the stigmata of the bullring. His Spanish paintings reek of sex and religiosity.

Rand came onto the scene in the late 80s, as we were winding down from the all-night ravages of a decade-long party. My contribution was a gallery called FUN. Underground film star Patti Astor and I started it in 1980 as a way to prolong the cocktail hour and incidentally, to show the work of a few friends. These included Basquiat, Keith Haring, and some legends of the graffiti world: Futura, Lee, Dondi. When the limos started pulling up, we knew the fun was over, and the work had begun. The spontaneous combustion of art and music and raw talent degenerated into a typical New York affectation of self-conscious preening. Who can be original when Andy Warhol is peering over your shoulder whispering "fabulous." Who can be real when you're having cocktails with Paul Simon at the Carlyle Hotel before the opening of the Whitney Biennial? The banquet in those days started at Odeon and finished at Mr. Chow, where Julian Schnabel, Francesco Clemente and Jean-Michel Basquiat supplicated themselves at the feet of Rene Ricard.

Rene Ricard was the thread that held this plot together. He was a poet. If he had been a goddess, he would have been Kali. If he'd been a princess, he would have been Margaret. If he'd been a queen... well, as he once wrote: *Queens are just Kings dressed up in heels.* Over the years, Ricard applied that heel assiduously to the forehead of the New York art world. As its transgressive king, you either worshipped him or walked the plank, usually on the pages of *Artforum.* Fortunately, the artists of FUN amused him, and we prospered.

The end of the 80s was the cool ash of a hot burn. Rene's apartment had literally gone up in flames, and he was alternately sleeping on the subway or in Jacqueline Schnabel's guest room. Basquiat and Haring were dead. Patti Astor was living in Hollywood, and I was sitting in the gallery at 56 Bleecker. The couch there became Rene's default throne. Where FUN Gallery had been optimistic and exuberant, the mood on Bleecker Street was darker. Stephen Sprouse painted the gallery black and chained his silkscreens to the wall. David LaChapelle showed intensely personal photographs exploring themes of AIDS and religion. Other Bleecker Gallery artists, like Elizabeth Peyton and William Rand, applied paint to canvas, pulling images out of an old medium that were startling and fresh. Peyton makes rock stars look like Caravaggio's rough trade, and Rand takes street hustlers and transforms them into rock stars.

Les Lecons des Tenebres, perhaps Rene Ricard's most uncanny and perfect piece of writing, was written for Rand's 1989 exhibition at 56 Bleecker Gallery, which I curated. It was reprinted in the catalog for Rand's large solo exhibition at the Colby College Museum of Art, which I also curated, together with museum director Hugh Gourley, in 1993.

Bill Stelling
Curator and Gallerist
Manchester, New Hampshire
December, 2017

How do we equate our knowledge of horror into modern, that is to say, terms, we can understand? In the seventeenth century the Bible offered incidents that were tremendous occasions for horror painting and the Cloaca Maxima – the massacre of the innocents, of church fathers, or in simpler terms, the passion of Christ. Since we live in an age stripped of codpieces and halberds, where the Capulets and Montagues are infrequently dashing swords in Astor Place, what is the iconography of horror and the occasions of pathos where the dreadful martyrdom is running its course? The torturer's horse is scratching its innocent behind on a tree.

There's a Latin quotation – Taceant colloquia effugiat risus hic locus est ubi mors gaudet succurrere vitae – (who the author is escapes me) over the entrance of the morgue on First Avenue more or less to the effect that one can learn more about a person when they're dead than when they're alive.

In William Rand's paintings for example one must look to the shadows for information. In fact this oeuvre is a meditation on darkness: a painting in the shade.

The dark bears a perjorative connotation in English as darkness is universally considered the abode of the dead and therefore fearsome. "The day of his death was a dark cold day" (Auden). Our perjorative inferrence from the dark relates to the dark as home of the shades, that is the dead, and necromania is putatively evil. Evil is a curious word; it only seems to exist in English: the dead on a mission. Evil cannot be expressed, for instance in French; 'Mal' is as bad as it gets: Mal de Mer: Seasickness to Fleur du "mal" is too general to be downright "Evil." To transport the diabolical freight of 'Evil' one must go straight to hell with 'Diabolique' and that word has too much capework for daily use.

Opposite:
N.C. (detail), 1992
Oil and linseed oil on canvas
62" x 56"

Courting the Dead with necromancy would seem to be the prerogative of Evil; for some reason we seek the dead at night. The use of the dead, however, is only 'Evil' in English. Relinquishing the dead to heaven and hell should take care of them, but since there are folks who actively seek the dead, and since the 'Good' dead are presumably off harping around the Throne; it is the restless dead below who have time for earthly vanities.

Using the dead is always fearsome; 'Evil' is something else. Anyone with invisible companions is shady to be sure but many civilizations put such awful talent to use: the Yoruba for instance.

In paint darkness must be represented with black paint and here again our cultural prejudices limit and condition our experience of the dark. White as 'Good' and black as 'Evil' has limited application in the realm of absolutes. On a grander scale it would seem that the opposite is truer: Black epidigmatic as it is of the Womb, the dark well from which truth springs and the color of most of the inhabitants of Washington D.C. is perhaps preferable as the color of viability, parties taking place as they do at night. I hesitate to use the words 'Good' and 'Evil' here as the dichotomy of black and white require subtler distinctions to extricate them from their linguistic bias: 'A black heart.'

I saw a show on educational TV a few years back that illustrates this to perfection.

The penetration of innermost New Guinea occurred sometime around the late 'Twenties, and was fully documented as a historical event by the film crew that came along for the plane ride with the, you guessed it, prospectors on a gold hunt. The indigenes who inhabited the mountainous terrain, clung clan by clan to their respective mountainsides – occasional raids and forays into the neighboring hillside being the extent of their gregariousness – were not nonplussed to see a giant bird descending into their midst to disgorge half the inventory of Abercrombie and Fitch, Kodak, and the Royal Society of Explorers.

The tack of the program I saw was, and this is genius, to interview the same people we saw in the earlier footage be-masked and mud-bedecked at their first encounter with Empire's vanguard, circa now as to what their reaction was to the invasion.

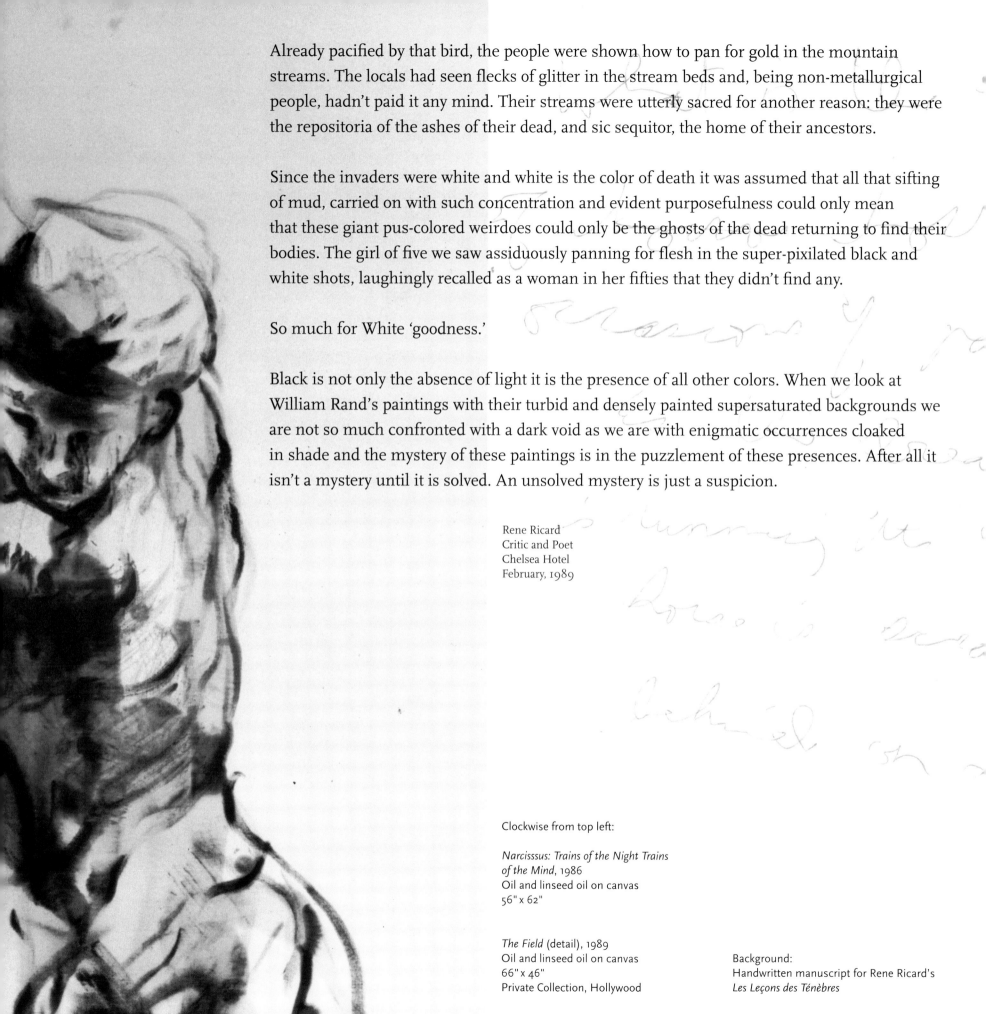

Already pacified by that bird, the people were shown how to pan for gold in the mountain streams. The locals had seen flecks of glitter in the stream beds and, being non-metallurgical people, hadn't paid it any mind. Their streams were utterly sacred for another reason: they were the repositoria of the ashes of their dead, and sic sequitor, the home of their ancestors.

Since the invaders were white and white is the color of death it was assumed that all that sifting of mud, carried on with such concentration and evident purposefulness could only mean that these giant pus-colored weirdoes could only be the ghosts of the dead returning to find their bodies. The girl of five we saw assiduously panning for flesh in the super-pixilated black and white shots, laughingly recalled as a woman in her fifties that they didn't find any.

So much for White 'goodness.'

Black is not only the absence of light it is the presence of all other colors. When we look at William Rand's paintings with their turbid and densely painted supersaturated backgrounds we are not so much confronted with a dark void as we are with enigmatic occurrences cloaked in shade and the mystery of these paintings is in the puzzlement of these presences. After all it isn't a mystery until it is solved. An unsolved mystery is just a suspicion.

Rene Ricard
Critic and Poet
Chelsea Hotel
February, 1989

Clockwise from top left:

Narcisssus: Trains of the Night Trains of the Mind, 1986
Oil and linseed oil on canvas
56" x 62"

The Field (detail), 1989
Oil and linseed oil on canvas
66" x 46"
Private Collection, Hollywood

Background:
Handwritten manuscript for Rene Ricard's
Les Leçons des Ténèbres

New York

William Rand studio,
East Village, New York, 1996

1960s-70s

In and out of the city, Rand absorbs the graphic environment: vivid Pop in the 60s; grungy, tattered Punk in the 70s; and the new, cool spray graffiti adorning subways cars and stations, which set a tone for the 80s.

1980s

First painting in room 1003, the "tower room," at the Hotel Chelsea, Rand moves to a floor-through loft on the corner of 1st Avenue and 1st Street in the East Village. His dark, dense Maine palette is supplanted by a lighter ground, and he scales up the size of his figures and faces.

1989

Rene Ricard, official poet of DIA Art Foundation, writes *Les Leçons des Ténèbres* for Rand's solo show and catalog at 56 Bleecker Gallery LTD, New York, New York.

A brilliant critic and poet, Ricard wrote about only a handful of painters, including Jean Michel Basquiat, Francesco Clemente, Brice Marden, Judy Rifka, Julian Schnabel, and William Rand.

1990

The Farnsworth Museum in Rockland, Maine features Rand in its *Voyages of the Modern Imagination*.

1992

Rand and Mead exhibit at Gotham Book Mart and Thread Waxing Space, New York, New York.

1993

William Rand solo exhibition at the Colby College Museum of Art in Waterville, Maine.

William Rand, *Self Portrait*, Carbon paper transfer drawing, 1991

National and International Events

1984
Jorg Immendorff paintings are exhibited at Mary Boone Gallery

1987
Andy Warhol dies after surgery

1988
Punk and Neo-Expressionist artist Jean-Michel Basquiat dies of a drug overdose

1989
I.M. Pei's pyramidal entrance to the Louvre opens to the public

1990
Beginning of the Human Genome Project

1991
Kuwaiti oil facilities are destroyed by Iraqi forces

1992
Los Angeles riots follow acquittal of police responsible for Rodney King assault

William Rand, photographed by
Timothy Greenfield-Sanders,
New York, 1982
From the series *Art World*
Collection of MoMA, New York, New York
and Museum of Fine Arts, Houston, Texas

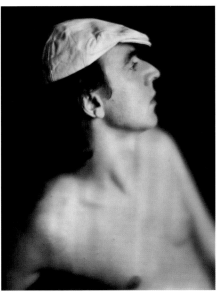

Rene Ricard, photographed by
Timothy Greenfield-Sanders,
New York, 1981
From the series *Art World*
Collection of MoMA, New York, New York
and Museum of Fine Arts, Houston, Texas

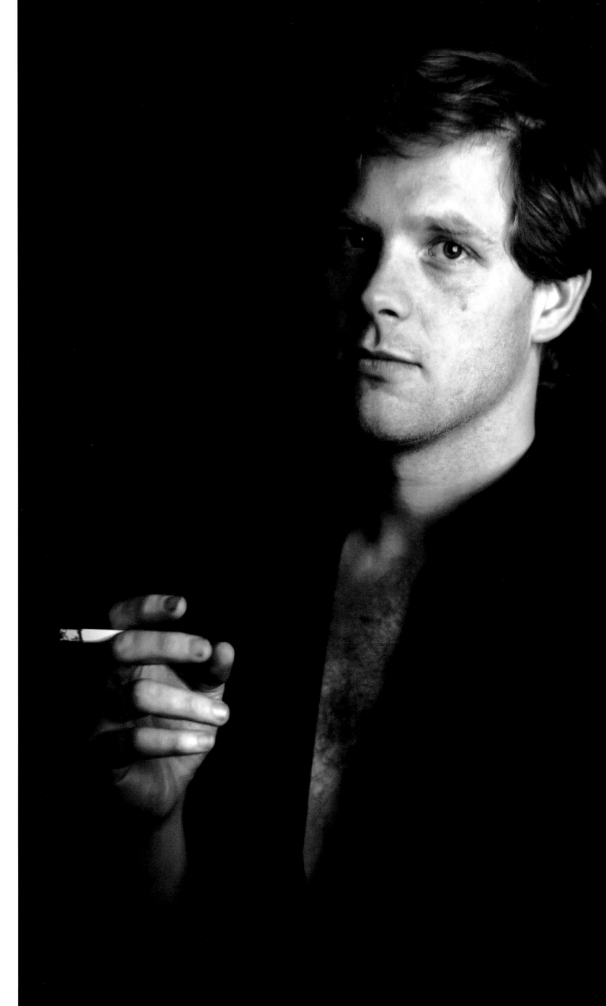

Annette, 1987
Oil on canvas
72" x 45"
Private Collection, Boston

**Black is not only the absence of light
it is the presence of all other colors...**

Rene Ricard

William Rand, Rene Ricard and Edward Brezinski
The World is My Oyster, Peel Me a Grape, 1989
Oil on canvas
72" x 72"
Coutesy of half gallery, New York

Rene Ricard, 1989
William Rand Studio
East Village, New York

Objects and human forms share a weathered, angst-ridden quality. Each is a record of what the world has done to it, in a manner reminiscent of (though bearing no resemblance to) John Chamberlain's crushed cars.

They are painted in black, white and gray, a choice to create a concrete, economical statement without the distractions or sentimentality of color, which Rand attributes to the influence of the Fluxus artist Albert M. Fine. But the shadowy spectral world he portrays also draws on his own New England heritage – the ghosts of drowned Yankee sea captains with pearls for eyes inspire his work.

Press Release (excerpt)
Jeffery Goldberg
William Rand: Shakespeare
Suzan Cooper Gallery, New York, 1987
(First New York one-man show)

Stage Set, 1982
Oil on canvas
16" x 20"

MAKE NEW YORK YOUR VACATION CITY

William Rand drawing on Hotel Chelsea stationery, 1989

William Rand

Essay by Rene Ricard

Catalogue cover for 1989 exhibition
of paintings at 56 Bleeker Gallery Ltd.

NEW YORK POST Page Six

SUNDAY JUNE 18 1989

Hard lessons

PAINTER Bill Rand commissioned poet Rene Ricard to write an essay to be published in the catalog of his current show at the 56, Bleecker Gallery. "It's called 'Lessons of Shadows' and it's about the dangers that lurk in the dark," Rand told PAGE SIX. But Ricard never learned his own lessons. As he and Rand were walking on East Houston Street, the poet hollered at some neighborhood toughs, who then came over to teach them a lesson. "There were three of them on Rene and one on me," said Rand. "We had knives all around our necks. They went through our pockets and socks. We almost ended up in the morgue." Sometimes dangers lurk even when it isn't dark.

New York Post, 1989

Opposite:
Order and Chaos, 1989
Oil and linseed oil on canvas
60" x 60"
Private Collection, Hollywood

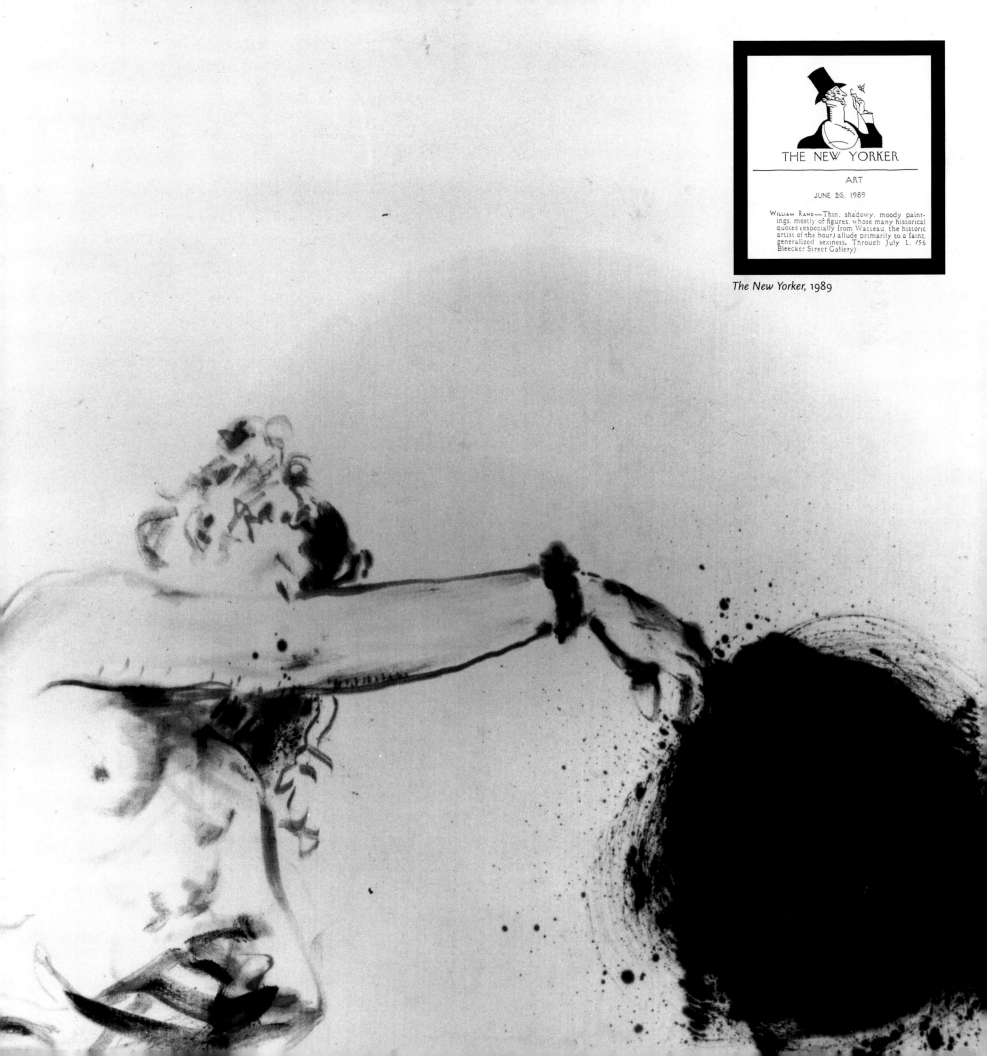

The New Yorker, 1989

Taylor Mead and William Rand,
New York, New York, 1991.

WILLIAM RAND
72 East First Street · New York, NY 10003 ☎ 420-1922

Press Release - Taylor Mead/William Rand Print Folio

This 1990 portfolio is a collaboration consisting of beat poems by Taylor Mead and powerful images by the New York artist William Rand. The poems, taken from Mead's *The Anonymous Diary of a New York Youth* (volumes 1 and 2), were originally published in 1960. (The five prints, each measuring 44" x 30", are available in an edition of 14).

Written and read on the beaches and in the coffeehouses on both coasts, Taylor Mead's poetry is as freewheeling and irresistible as his screen performances of the period, such as Ron Rice's pioneering film *The Flower Thief* and Vernon Zimmerman's *Lemon Hearts* (MOMA Rosenthal Award), in which Mead plays eight roles.

In the fifties it became clear that the authorities were going in the wrong direction. The beat philosophy was bold in its reaction to the rigid cold war political climate. We more or less followed Kerouac and Ginsberg's dictum that 'first thoughts best thoughts.'

Summing up his film work, Mead explains:

We were revolting against The Brady Bunch *and their contrived scripts.*

The Mead/Rand prints were exhibited in 1992 at the Gotham Book Mart and the Thread Waxing Space, where, at the exhibition's opening, Mead shared a poetry reading with Rene Ricard.

The prints are included in the following collections: Colby College Museum of Art, Farnsworth Museum and Library, and the New York Public Library Print Collection.

I've stolen God,
I put him in my pocket and squeezed him.
All the juices are flowing all over the beaches
And the acid from ....

The Anonoymous Diary of a New York Youth
From Taylor Mead/William Rand Print Folio, 1990
44" x 30"
Collection of the New York Public Library

Taylor Mead and William Rand
New York, New York, 1986.

Giancarlo Reading, 1994
Mixed media on canvas
280" x 140"

Giancarlo

Painting in East Villge studio,
New York, New York, 1994

The artist seeks the archetype.

That which is invisible acts upon the artistic psyche, call it romanticism, because the artist is incomplete without it.

A painting can begin months before brush touches canvas, and the creation of an image that has never existed before, turns into something of a sign, which has been pre-destined, as if it had always been here.

It is the sign of the monster.

The gestalt is the arrival of the messenger into the present.

It returns from the past and the future, wearing the glistening badge of entitlement and authenticity, and that is art´s destiny.

Models can trigger this anxiety.

The first time I saw Giancarlo in New York I knew I would paint him.

The black shiny icicles of Sicilian hair showering down over his face, the heavy thudding motorcycle boots, the delicate fingers and his understated Mona Lisa smile were gracefully thrown around the cryptic fires of his eyes, ancient fires of Roman encampments reflected in the Nile's treacherous waters, the same waters that drowned Antinoos.

When this happens one can only begin painting, and painting and painting because the current is very strong there.

WILLIAM RAND, NEW YORK, 1994

Medic, 1992
Gesso, charcoal, oil, lead, latex on canvas
72" x 72"

Blut und Boden, 1993
Oil on canvas
68" x 72"

Maine Times, 1993

The paintings of William Rand, who lives in New York and Gouldsboro Maine, root the vocabulary of violence in the culture of photojournalism and mass media. In his just-ended show at Colby, a series of black and white works on paper charged one wall with a non-stop history of Western machismo. Baseball players, military parades, scientific diagrams and suits of armour crowded into a nightmarish montage of photos and drawings. Some of these images found their way into large black and white paintings, anchored in a sketchy chiaroscuro way that imparted a hurried feel, as if these were visions he just had to get down fast, a kind of exorcism.

Rand conveys a mythology of aggression without glorifying it. His works try to tell the truth about pain and horror that men both face and inflict; they name evils yet don't inspire sympathy. Instead, Rand gives us a shadowy-if not shady-view of maleness as familiar as the evening news.

Haines Sprunt Tate
Maine Times, Review of William Rand Exhibition
Colby College Museum of Art, 1993

Tonight

Tomorrow never comes
not when it's tonight

Night
This night.
Night of sighs
Avenue of lights

Love can sneak up on you.
The distant strains of hungry dreams
seem pointless
when you hit the wall at these speeds
you'll sleep with a brick as a pillow.
Robert Frost on the subject
of promises to keep.

Wm. Rand 1994

Julie and friends at the Whitney, 1995
Enamel paint on collaged canvas
84" x 84"

In medieval art people tended to be extreme caricatures of social class: social cloning and stereotype are also fundamental to the Rand Pantheon. Conflicts of public versus personal honor are recycled in an age of duty and doubt.

History repeats itself as farce. Borges reminds us, the circular structure older than the odyssey and growing more predictable and deranged as history unforgivingly recycles horror and cliche.

Allan Wallis, historian
William Rand Paintings
450 Broadway Gallery, New York, 1996

Rescue, 1992
Oil on reverse primed canvas
60" x 72"
Private Collection, New York

William Rand in New York studio, 1995

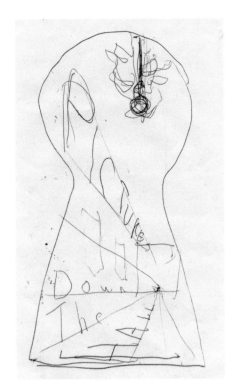

Rene Ricard
Drawing for William Rand, 1989
Ink on paper
11" x 8.5"

The Sugar Church -
A Portrait of Rene Ricard, 1992
Mixed media on canvas
72" x 58"

Giancarlo Writing, 1993
Charcoal, oil, varnish, and gesso on canvas
36" x 72"

Will (detail), 1993
Pencil, oil, charcoal, and gesso on linen
72" x 58"

William Rand sweeping studio floor,
New York, New York, 1995

Loves of Giancarlo, 1994
Mixed media on canvas
112" x 60"

I liked the large drawings by
William Rand – powerful, though nearly
enervated, symptomatic of
Generation X´s alibi of dependence on
media alibis.

Robert C. Morgan
Art critic

Cover, 1994

Avenging Angel, 1994
Mixed media on canvas
102" x 72"
Exhibited E.M. Donahue Gallery, New York, 1994
(Destroyed)

Over the years, I've watched William Rand's work go from maximal to minimal. His penchant for Baroque enhancement has been supplanted by a sleeker, more contemporary vocabulary in which multi-ethnic icons, the street gods of urban life, are fated to live out their epic tragedies and triumphs, a modern spin on classical narrative.

Bill Stelling, New York
Curator's Report:
William Rand Exhibition catalog
Colby College Museum of Art, Waterville, Maine, 1993

Suicide, Rikers Island, 1996
Charcoal, oil, and gesso on canvas
96" x 84"

William Rand and models,
New York, New York, 1995

William Rand with model Mei Ling and
Chinese studio assistants, 1996

New York Late Night Poem

Night life, rain and the blue police car crossing the rain soaked bridge.
I am painting your eyelash. The brush finds the reflection of the window in the retina,
and the F Train rumbles underground.

Opposite:
William Rand in Magic Gallery,
East Berlin, 1990

Der Soldat A Tragic Dionysian Artist

Bullet Hole, Bode Museum, 1990

The artist William Rand exhibited *Der Soldat* in the autumn of 1990 in the Magic Gallery in East Berlin. This was one year after the fall of the wall in the heart of Berlin-Mitte, the museum island, where the most important art in Berlin is displayed — in the Bode Museum, Pergamon Museum, Altes Museum, Neues Museum, Alte National Galerie, Ägyptisches Museum.

Der Soldat represents the duality of war and peace after the fall of the Berlin wall. The artist wants to show us "the blessedness" (die Seligkeit), as well as the nihilistic values of a people affected by the last war and post-war peace. It contains the tones of the ever-pregnant music of Richard Wagner, which can still be heard after the war. It evokes Schopenhauer and Nietzsche: their ideas of art as the liberator of knowledge; the intensification of the will to live and creation in "future humans," or Übermenschen. It suggests creative artists struggling amidst nihilism, vitalism, and existentialism.

And so *Der Soldat* is a tragic, or conflicted, Dionysian artist, a symbol of both war and its opposite. The painting portrays life, the will to live, and the permanence of creative expression as an affirmation of Nietzsche's concept of the "eternal return."

Dr. Silvia Silveira Laguna
Doctor in Philosophy
Editorial Laguna

Thoughts from my book
Der Wille zur Macht als Kunst (The Will to Power as Art)
Berlin, 15 September 2017
With much love for my friend William Rand

Translated from German by Helen Cafferty

1989

Rand travels by rail from Koln to Berlin. The passing German landscape reveals violent damage from the war.

Old wooden cattle cars left from the Holocaust stand in train yards, full of potatoes: "Vergangenheitsbewaeltigung."

Rand and bohemian artist Edward Brezinski paint in a large studio under a nightclub, entering the shady milieu of all-night Berlin. During the day, they sketch in Café Einstein.

Walking outside the battered, solitary Reichstag, they discover people climbing over the wall – a profoundly historic moment.

The crushed brick and stone ground they walk on is the pulverized rubble of bombed buildings.

Excerpts from the artist's Berlin diaries, 1989

1990

Rand exhibits with Brezinski at Magic Gallery, 17-10-90 Rykestrasse, 22 Ost (East) Berlin.

The gallery, dank and candle lit, is located in a squat within a series of abandoned buildings. Politicians, nobility, and art-world stars are in attendance.

The two artists install themselves in the Bode Museum. Rand explores "no-man's land" by the remains of the Berlin Wall at dawn. German ravens swoop back and forth between the branches of the leafless trees, screeching: "We saw it all! We saw it all!"

National and International Events

1988
The first World Aids Day is held in December.

Picasso's *Acrobat & Harlequin* sells for $37.6 million at auction in England.

1989
Robert Mapplethorpe dies.

Idi Amin is expelled from Zaire.

O.J. Simpson pleads no contest to battering his wife, Nicole Simpson, during a New Year's Day argument.

Pro-democracy rallies in Tiananmen Square

Earthquake in San Francisco

Tanker Exxon Valdez strikes a reef and releases 11 million gallons of oil into Alaska's Prince William Sound

1990
Keith Haring dies.

Launch of the Hubble Space Telescope

Right: *Untitled*, 1990
Collage
10" x 6.25"

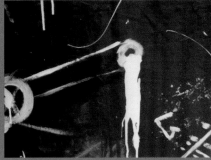

Untitled, 1990
Collage
10" x 6.25"

Weathervane, 1990
Mixed media on canvas
48" x 72"
Private Collection, Berlin

Edward BREZINSKI
und William RAND

AUSSTELLUNGSERÖFFNUNG
11·10·90
18°° – 20°° UHR

Magic Gallery
Rykestrasse 22
Ost Berlin

Exhibition Poster, 1990
Poster concept and design by
William Rand and Julie Jo Fehrle
Offset Lithography
17" x 11"

Berlin, Germany

November 17, 1989

Painting until dawn with a friend in the abandoned basement of a West Berlin nightclub, the 15 foot wide brown and green oil painting we have been working on is of some singular witchcraft incident in the Black Forest.

It has become a monstrous sea of thrashing muck.

Pine trees grow muscular arms dripping with paint and trembling in the candle light and my friend has been talking backwards for half an hour.

Leading him up to the street, he faints onto the hard damp blue German cobblestones from exhaustion and lack of food. I have only just arrived by train from Koln.

I lift his lifeless body into my arms and standing up, all around us are flower carts bursting with flowers, and the faces of hardened German women staring blandly, like the flowers, at nothing. We are drowning in the flower market at dawn and I do not know where to go.

Turning around and around I can see figures climbing up on a distant wall and men are shouting.

All I can see are thousands of flowers as the mighty sun rises that morning in Berlin.

He stirs, nodding, and points up a street. Coming to his senses he can suddenly walk. Lighting up a smoke, he begins speaking German casually, as if nothing had happened at all.

WILLIAM RAND

East Berlin, 1991

Opposite:
Hymn, 1998
Mixed media on fifteen canvases, assembled
54" x 54"

El Punto De Las Bellas Artes
November, 1997
Espacio Pepe Rubio Madrid

Se trata de cuadros de gran formato en los que aparecen, agilmente dibujados con pintura gris y negra, una serie de rostros o de figuras en un contexto de signos y de fragmentos. Diriase que se trata de dibujos a tinta china ampliados, dibujos en los que se ha tratado de reproducir el trazo del ilustrador, la calidad del dibujo publicitario. Los personajes podrian tambien ser modelos: jovenes con hermosos rostros que evolucionan en un contexto de tension y de violencia, entre vertiginosos disenos y explosiones de pintura. Es un mundo vivo, trepidante, en el que se confunden el cine y la realidad, el simbolo y el diseno, el amor y la violencia, que el pintor plasma con eficacia en cuadros que se imponen por si mismos.

Angels, 1987-1997
Assembled drawings on board
18" x 18" (Drawing size)

Looking for work at the Opera, 1997
Acrylic on four canvases, assembled
36" x 48"

Matador (detail), 1997
Mixed media on
nine canvases, assembled
60" x 48"
Private Collection, Madrid

1996

Rand moves to Europe, opening a studio in the Chueca barrio of Madrid.

He moves quickly through the late 90s Spanish gold rush, painting and drawing large format dibujos (drawings) on linen and executing portrait commissions.

1999

The artist exhibits a series based on 18th-century French drawings in the Barrio de Salamanca, Madrid

El artista trabaja con lo minimo para dejar al desnudo sus maximas posibles formales, un milagro que solo se opera en la mas dolorosa y humilde voluntad del arte, la que siempre estuvo alejada del ajetreado y vicioso circulo de su mercadeo: lograr mucho con muy, muy poco.

Ines Lopez-Quesada, Comisario
William Rand Galeria Cuatro Diecisiete-Madrid, 1999

2000

Rand moves to El Rastro in La Latina, Madrid.

2001

Rand opens a second atelier in El Rastro to house his paintings and keeps producing new work.

2002

Rand writes the introduction to a catalog for the Madrid exhibition of a New York colleague, Canadian artist Graham Gillmore:

The Valley of the Words: Graham Gillmore
Essay by William Rand, May, 2002
Published by Galeria Fucares

2000-2003

Using trans-Atlantic letters (the last of air mail before the internet kicks in), New York poet and Neo-Geo art critic Richard Milazzo collaborates with Rand on *The Ava Gardner Project*. The vast interchangeable mural, dark and passionate, like the subterranean Spanish lifestyle of the actress, becomes an unholy vision of the decadent 50s and a violent destruction of glamour.

2003

Galeria Najera presents William Rand's *The Modular Ava Gardner* with catalog essay by Milazzo.

At the opening, massive klieg lights on either side of the gallery doors face the historic Puerta de Alcala, the 18th-century Roman Revival stone arch still bullet-ridden from the Spanish Civil War.

2005

Rand moves to the Spanish Mediterranean, opening a studio in Alicante.

Small Works
William Rand studio, Spain, 2005

2006

He illustrates *Billy Budd* by Herman Melville with small drawings, and paints *Los Marineros*. His painting *The Petroleum Springtime* features sinister, sexy frogmen, who loot ancient Roman busts of Caesar from war-torn oil fields.

2008

Poet in New York and *Valley of the Dolls* painting and drawing catalogs are published, encompassing Rand's work from Madrid and the Mediterranean.

Rand's models include prostitutes from the local bordello, Russian kick boxers, teenage bodybuilders, strippers, international club kids, surfers, "toughs," Moroccans, and John the Baptist. He paints gladiators, carefree girls in bikinis, Saint Augustine, a baseball player, Antinoos, and Hamlet.

On the other side of the Mediterranean, military conflict is never far away.

Rand takes time to write in Marrakech, Tangiers and Istanbul, working on his New York diaries from the 80s and 90s.

2009

El Palacio de Congressos de Alicante acquires a painting by Rand after his solo exhibition there. The Portland Museum of Art also acquires one.

Rand's geometric Bahnhof series draws on cold war memories of German train stations.

2013-2014

By the beach, Rand paints a large, monochromatic, twelve-part WWII mural titled *1945*, a modular *Gates of Hell*.

Rene Ricard dies in New York.

2015

Rand closes his Mediterranean studio and ships 225 wooden crates of paintings by boat from Valencia to Boston Harbor.

Calle San Marcos, Chueca, 1997
Acrylic on canvas
48" x 68"

National and International Events

1996
Cuba downs two American planes.

1998
Jackson Pollock retrospective exhibition at the Museum of Modern Art.

1999
The German Bundestag returns to Berlin.

2001
On 9/11, terrorist attacks on the World Trade Center kill 3,000 people.

2002
Nan Goldin's *El Patio del Diablo* is exhibited at Palacio de Velazquez, Parque del Retiro, Madrid.

2003
U.S.-led coalition launches an invasion of Iraq.

2004
Terrorists explode simultaneous bombs on Madrid's rail network, ripping through a commuter train, rocking three stations, and killing 190.

William Rand, El Rastro studio courtyard, Madrid, 2001

Death in the Afternoon, 2001
Oil on nine canvases, assembled
77" x 65"
Private Collection, Madrid

Water Nymph, 1997
Pencil on paper
10" x 8"

2006
The Deep Space Network makes a final attempt to contact Pioneer 10, but no response is received.

The artist's father dies in Scarborough, Maine.

2009
In Germany, the building of the Historisches Archiv der Stadt Koln collapses.

2012
The Mesoamerican Long Count Calendar reaches the date 13.0.0.0.0.

2014
A deadly outbreak of Ebola in West Africa sparks a global health crisis.

Malaysia Airlines Flight 370 disappears between Kuala Lampur and Beijing.

2015
Terrorist target the offices of French satirical newspaper *Charlie Hebdo*

Supreme Court allows same-sex couples to marry nationwide.

Tens of thousands flee war-torn Syria.

Top: *Rogue Cop,* 1997
Oil on canvas
60" x 72"
Private Collection, Madrid

Middle: *Drummer,* 1997
Oil on canvas
60" x 72"
(Stolen in Paris)

Bottom: *Thug,* 1997
Oil on canvas
60" x 72"
(Stolen in Paris)

New Math, 1997
Oil on canvas
48" x 36"
Private Collection, Canada

The shadow of a giant scarab
covers Madrid,
twisting slowly against the dawn.

William Rand
Studio notes
Spain, 1997

The Diamond Thief, 1997
Latex on twelve canvases, assembled
54.5" x 60"

Primavera (Springtime), 1998
Oil on canvas
60" x 60"
Private Collection, Washington, D.C.

William Rand studio wall, Madrid, 1998

White Bonsai (Salome), 1999
Latex, acrylic, oil stick on linen
with magic marker
36" x 60"
Private Collection, Madrid

Black Bonsai, 1999
Latex, acrylic, oil stick on linen
with magic marker
36" x 60"
Private Collection, Madrid

Opposite:
Ava-Mediteranean (detail), 2003
Oil on canvas
38" x 64"
Private Collection, Los Angeles

Modular Ava Gardner,
2000-2003
Acrylic, oil, oil stick,
varnish, Coca-Cola,
coffee, red wine, salt,
eyeliner, glitter, spray
paint, dirt, pencil, etc.
36" x 36" each

Royal Palace, 2003
Acrylic on cloth
35" x 40"
Private Collection, New Hampshire

Royal Palace, 2004
Latex on wood panel
58.5" x 44.5"
Private Collection, Madrid

**The most beautiful animal
in a very ugly world**

A large modular mural of
interchangeable square
paintings, this Guernica of
human self-destruction is a
"torbellino" of black and white
images, a voyage to the
end of Ava Gardner's Spanish
night revealing the darkest
side of glamour, desire
and frustration, sexual anxiety,

voraciousness and dissatisfac-
tion. But also the shine and
the uncorruptability of beauty
in the dark landscape of
Fascist Spain in the 1950s."

Felix Leiro, film critic

"Corazon de Madrid, Viva la Vida"
El Mundo
14 Septiembre, 2002

*William Rand Exhibition
Ava Gardner, Sacred and Profane*
Galeria Najera
Plaza de la Independencia
Madrid

Asdrubal, 2004-2005
Mixed media on six canvases,
assembled
68" x 48"

Nancy Area

I had met Nancy in Madrid, and she was a Moroccan streetwalke
who loved club music and would always make dramatic leg
splitting geometric entrances whenever she appeared in public.
Her dancing often involved blocking doors, handstands,
pirouettes and other circus tricks from a provincial desert
roadshow.

Nancy was his stage name.
A saltimbanque, she would pose in front of my large paintings
at the underground nightclub late at night in Madrid,
as if they were a backdrop for her acrobatic side-show.
She sought out the spotlight, and the fastest songs made her
slow down.

She made cash on the side posing for an elderly blind painter
in El Rastro, who for some reason always painted Nancy
in abstract triangles, triangles that overlapped.

The Petroleum Springtime, 2006
Mixed media on canvas
48" x 21.25"

Opposite:
Billy Budd (Los Marineros), 2005
Carbon paper transfer drawings on
various paper types with wash
8.5" x 8.5"

By the Sea, 2007
Mixed media on eight canvases, assembled
55" x 142"

Natasha Bound, 2007
Mixed media on four canvases, assembled
55" x 71"

Sexual Tourism, 2007
Mixed media on four canvases, assembled
55" x 71"

Joint Checking, 2011
Oil on four canvases, assembled
64" x 52"

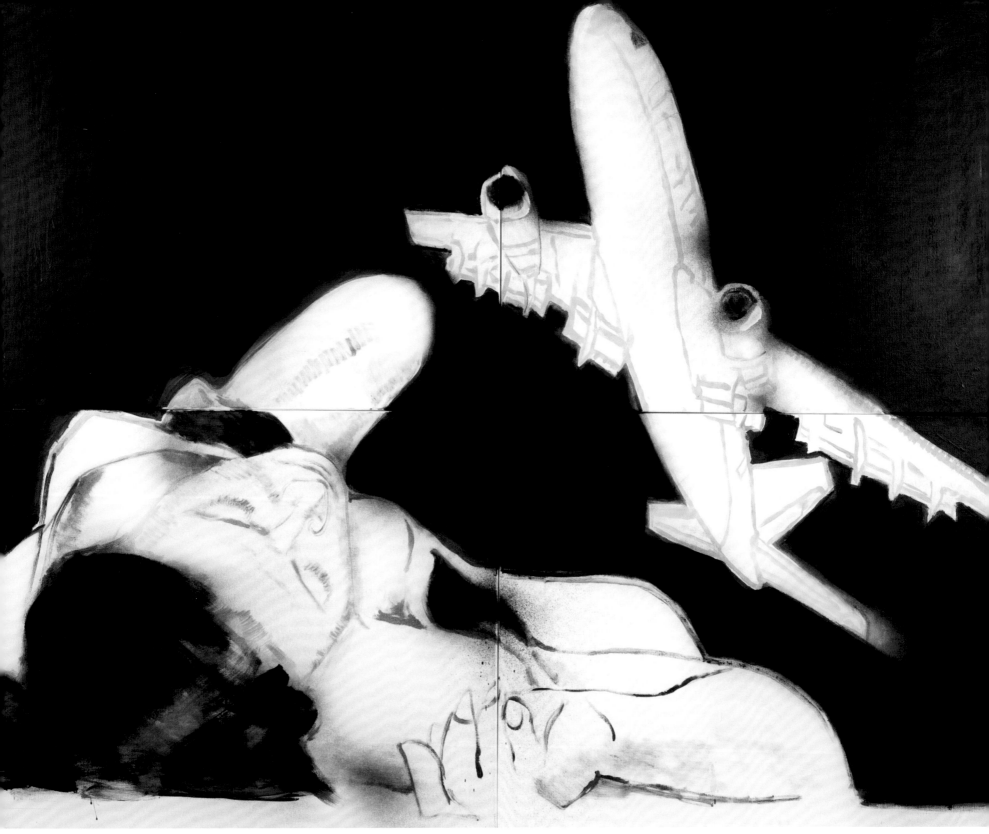

Runway 49, 2007
Oil on four canvases, assembled
52" x 64"

Passing Clouds (detail), 2010
Acrylic on four canvases, assembled
56" x 70"

Drummer, 2011
Mixed media on four canvases, assembled
72" x 57"

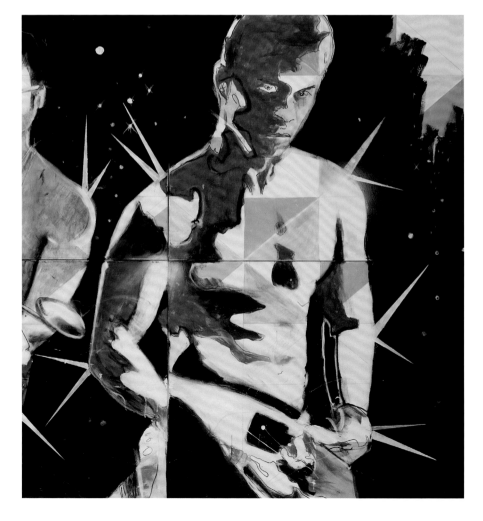

Tex Mex (detail), 2009
Mixed media on four canvases, assembled
72" x 57"

The swan is not dedicated to Apollo without cause, because forseeing his happiness in dea

dies singing with pleasure. Cicero

Smoke, 2009
Oil on canvas
114" x 62"

Oblivion, 2013
Mixed media on canvas
76" x 59"

The Baroness, 2013
Mixed media on canvas
76" x 59"

Bahnhof IV, 2013
Mixed media on four canvases, assembled
146" x 184"

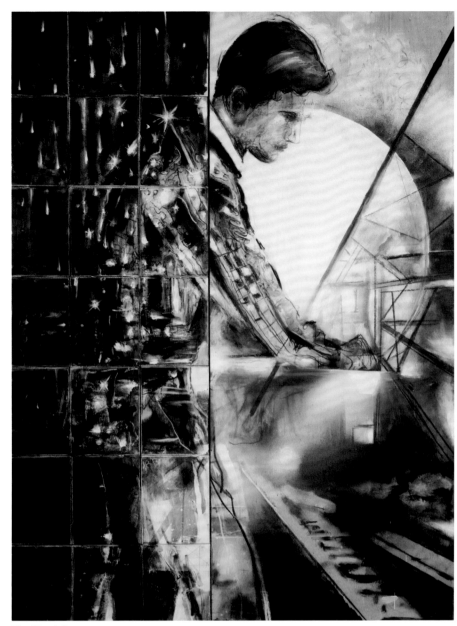

The Wood Carpenter, 2014
Mixed media on twenty-one canvases and
one wood panel, assembled
70" x 53"

Alone - Tangier, 2014
Mixed media on canvas
76" x 59"

Winter, 2014
Mixed media on canvas
76" x 59"

Opposite:
The Guest Mooring (detail), 2017
Mixed media on twelve canvases, assembled
65" x 60"

Studio notes (detail), 2018
Mixed media on 8" x 8" canvases

2016

The artist returns to Maine.

Rand sees old America as the source of the great tragic themes haunting the nation: war, slavery, women's rights, social injustice and suffering. He ultimately settles upon the hooded figure of death as a complicit symbol of human destiny.

2017

Rand paints scaled-up images on canvas and collages large images printed in black and white on wood, thus fulfilling the poet Rene Ricard's 1995 prediction that Rand would eventually become an "affichiste."

Requiring extra large prints with specific measurements to fit large wooden supports, Rand works closely with Staples staff in Maine and New York and explores more violent and gestural means of gluing the large print-outs.

Maynard Monrow and Bill Stelling curate an exhibition, *Love Among the Ruins*, at Howl in New York City, featuring *The Sugar Church: A Portrait of Rene Ricard*, 1992 by William Rand.

National and International Events

2016

Bashar al-Assad employs barrel bombs and chemical weapons in response to citizen revolt, and the Syrian refugee crisis begins.

Brazil and South Korea impeach their presidents.

Terrorists launch major attacks in Nice, Belgium, Pakistan, and Orlando.

Russia interferes in the U.S. presidential election.

2017

North Korea fires ballistic missile tests across the Sea of Japan.

Ai Weiwei's *Good Fences Make Good Neighbours* public art projects are unveiled in Manhattan

Mass killings, systematic rape, and torture of the Rohingya minority in Myanmar.

U.S. military launches 59 Tomahawk cruise missiles at an air base in Syria in response to a suspected chemical weapons attack on a rebel-held town.

Proposed removal of Confederate statues prompts KKK rally in Charlottesville, Virginia

Club 57 exhibit at MoMA showcases East Village artists and musicians of the late 70s and early 80s.

Sony Music Entertainment begins to press vinyl records again after a three-decade hiatus.

Sexual harrassment charges against prominent media, political, and business figures spark the #metoo movement.

Ice jam on Kennebec River floods parts of Hallowell and Augusta, Maine.

2018

The artist's mother dies in South Freeport, Maine.

A mass shooting at Marjory Stoneman Douglas High School in Parkland, Florida kills seventeen students and teachers.

Firing Squad, 2017
Mixed media on six wood panels, assembled
108" x 179"

Maynard Monrow
Gesamt Kunst Werk, 2017
Mixed media
18" x 12"
Dedicated to William Rand

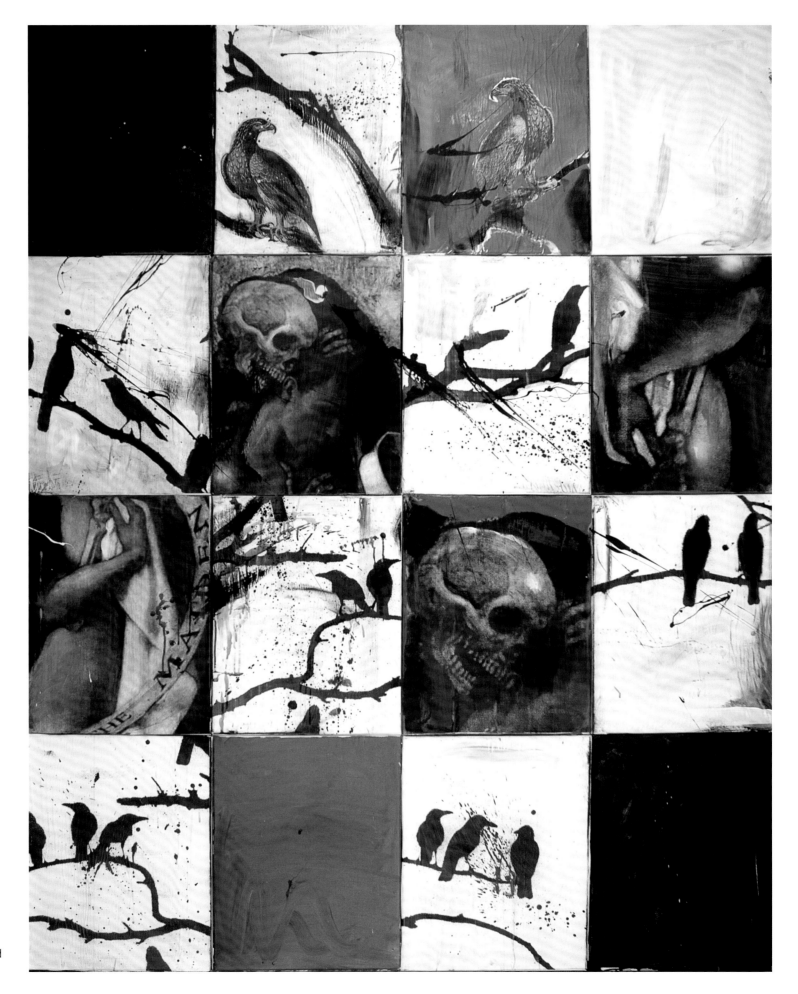

Winter Flowers, 2017
Mixed media on
sixteen canvases, assembled
80" x 64"

Within the image:
J. JIMENEZ ARANDA
UNA ESCLAVA EN VENTA

J. JIMÉNEZ ARANDA. Una esclava en venta. — Museo de Arte Moderno.

Begging Slave on the Dock, 2017
Mixed media on two wood panels,
dimensions variable
87" x 49"

Victor Hugo's Wife, 2017
Mixed media on three canvases,
dimensions variable
70" x 48"

I come from a long line of strong and noble ancestors. When I look upon William Rand's *The Long Walk*, I see them. I see their suffering, their subjugation, and their hope of overcoming the horrors of slavery.

The Long Walk, 2017
Mixed media on four wood panels, assembled
36" x 128"

But the figures in the painting –
tormented, murdered, perhaps
worse – also represent more
universal suffering, other types of
struggles, and other shackles
that bind us.

My ancestors' stories fortify me in my own life's journey, and the painting empowers me too.
I note the distance I've come from those tortured beginnings.

Runaway Slave with Cow, 2017
Collage and paint on three wood panels, assembled, dimensions variable
47" x 120"

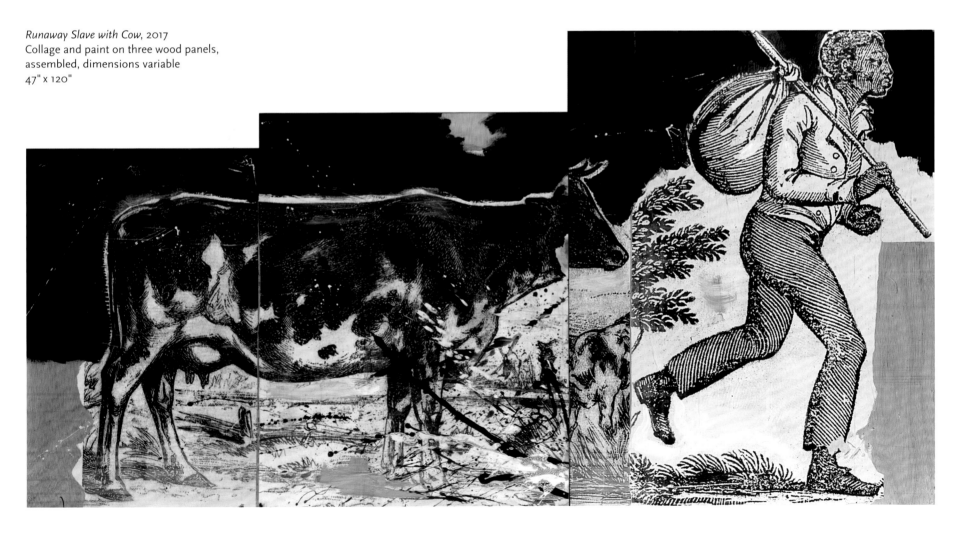

I'm able to see the goodness in people, regardless of the atrocities, physical and emotional, we inflict upon one another.

In the same way, this powerful piece does more than comment on "those poor people." It comments on the human race, whose members are sometimes more or less cognizant of human pain and sorrow. William Rand is in the former camp, and this book attests to his belief in the resilient human spirit.

Anthony Gaskin, educator, 2018

Crying Angels, 2017
Collage, oil on two wood panels, assembled,
dimensions variable
54" x 57"

The Architect, 2017
Mixed media on four wood panels, assembled
58" x 84"

Contributors

Credits

The contributors have long standing relationships with both the artist and his productions in Maine, New York, and Europe.

Special thanks to the estate of Haines Sprunt Tate and the *Maine Times*.

Special thanks to conceptual artist Maynard Monrow for his contribution.

Contributors' copyrights remain with respective authors and photographers.

Work with your friends.
Rene Ricard

Writing
Dennis Adamo
Cicero
Albert M. Fine
Anthony Gaskin
Jeffery Goldberg
Silvia Silviera Laguna
Felix Leiro
Ines Lopes-Quesada
Philip M. Isaacson
Suzette McAvoy
Taylor Mead
Robert C. Morgan
William Rand
Rene Ricard
Earle G. Shettleworth Jr.
Bill Stelling
Haines Sprunt Tate
Allan Wallis

Photography (documentation)
Sylvia Ball, 72
Edward Brezinski, 77
Lisa Dombek, 37
Julie Jo Fehrle, 83
Timothy Greenfield-Sanders, 49
Steven Guthrie, 2
Barbara Hawes, 17
Richard Knapp, 69
Charlotte L'Esperance, 73
Felix Leiro, 91
Mark Lyon, 27
Leslie Mackin, 14, 17, 56
Everett McCourt, 5, 64
William Baker Rand, 4, 17, 22, 24, 28, 35, 43, 48, 51, 59, 78, 79, 89, 95
John R. Rand, 8
Phil Rogers, 10, 38
Deborah Tripodi, 16
Ken Woisard, 30
Nick Wrathal, 56

Photography and Scanning (artwork)
Colby College Museum of Art, 86
Fine Arts Museums of San Francisco, 11
Antonio Garcia, 101-107, 109-113
Pedro Laguna, 84, 86-91, 93-100
Maynard Monrow, 118
Christine Olmstead, 18, 26, 56, 86, 115, 118-127
Portland Museum of Art, 13
Adam Reich, 41, 55
Ken Woisard, 20-22, 25, 28, 29, 31
Jason Wyche, 118
Brad Woodworth, 3, 42, 54, 61, 66, 74, 81, 91
Jay York, 36, 37

Published by Osprey Press LLC.
Copyright © 2018 William Rand/
Artists Rights Society (ARS), New York

All artwork is from the collection of William Baker Rand unless otherwise indicated.

Thank You
Leopoldo Alas
Elizabeth Cashin
Peter Hale
Raymond Foye
Pat Plourde
Santiago Avila Encina Rey

Editor
Amy E. Waterman

Design
Woodworth Associates

Typography
Scala, Scala Sans, and Scala Black

Printing
Penmor Lithographers
Edition of 500

ISBN: 978-0-692-07870-9

Cover:
The Guest Mooring (detail), 2017
Mixed media on twelve canvases, assembled
65" x 60"

Endurance is really the goal in art - drawing the essence out of everyday images to create icons that will last.

William Rand